The world is a great book, of which they who
never stir from home read only a page.
Augustine.

ETIQUETTE
for the
TRAVELLER

Compiled by
Beryl Peters

Copper Beech Publishing

Published in Great Britain by
Copper Beech Publishing Ltd
© Beryl Peters/Copper Beech Publishing Ltd 1999

Editor Jan Barnes

ISBN 1 898617 20-1

A CIP catalogue record for this book is available from the
British Library.

Copper Beech Publishing Ltd
P O Box 159 East Grinstead
Sussex England RH19 4FS

ETIQUETTE FOR THE TRAVELLER
CONTAINING

*There is nothing that a man can less afford
to leave at home than his conscience
or his good habits.*
Packe

*I cannot rest from travel;
I will drink life to the lees.*
Alfred Tennyson

Etiquette helps the wheels of life to turn smoothly and happily. It is especially important for travellers to know how to behave both in their own country and in foreign places.

A little knowledge enables one to give due consideration to others, to appear and to be at ease in all circumstances, to say and to do the right thing at the right time.

Remember that the spirit of true courtesy does not find expression only on social occasions but in everyday affairs such as travelling in public vehicles and walking in the streets whether at home or overseas.

FIRST RULES FOR TRAVELLERS

Money

Take one fourth more than your estimated expenses, and a good supply of small change.

Geography

Acquaint yourself with the geography of the route and region of travel.

Luggage

Arrange, if possible to have but one piece of luggage to look after.

Dress

Better be too hot for two or three hours at noon than be cold for the remainder of the twenty four.

Time

Under all circumstances be at the place of starting fifteen minutes before time, thus allowing for unanticipated detention by the way.

FIRST RULES FOR TRAVELLERS

Patience

Take with you a month's supply of patience, and always think thirteen times before you reply once to any supposed rudeness, insult or inattention.

Breakfast

Do not commence a day's travel before breakfast, even if it has to be eaten at day-break. Dinner or supper can be more healthily dispensed with than a good breakfast.

Manners

Respect yourself by exhibiting the manners of a gentleman or lady, if you wish to be treated as such, and then you will receive the respect of others.

A Good Luncheon Cake for Travellers.

Take half a pound of butter or dripping, three eggs, half a pound of brown sugar, one and a quarter pound of flour, quarter of a pound of candied peel, half a pound of sultanas, half a pint of milk, quarter of an ounce of carbonate of soda, pinch of tartaric acid. Mix the acid and soda with the flour, then rub in the fat, add the sugar, sultanas, and candid peel, beat the eggs well, warm the milk, add it to the eggs, then mix quickly with the other ingredients, put into a warm buttered tin and quickly into the oven. The oven should be rather hot and bake for about an hour and a half.

PREPARATION FOR TRAVEL

A good knowledge of the language ...

Behaviour when travelling is a sure indication of a person's breeding and a little preparation will make the journey more agreeable.

A good knowledge of the language of the country you are to visit is an immense help. The Emperor Charles V used to say that in proportion to the number of languages a man knew, he was so many more times a man.

'A knowledge of the language of the country you travel in is as good as a filled purse, as two pairs of eyes, as one pair of ears; for without it the one pair he possesses is likely to be of little use.'

CLIMATE

For longer journeys and to tropical climates ...

No special considerations may be necessary when travelling to temperate climates or on short journeys, but for longer journeys and to tropical climates, it is important that your servant arranges for tropical clothes to be part of your hand luggage.

The traveller's comfort relies on his dress being suitable to the climate he is in.

'Let us get between our hat and boots perpendicularly and be off.'

DRESS

... the importance of wearing flannel ...

A traveller should study comfort more than elegance, in the cut of his clothes, and little attention should be paid to change in fashion.

For a temperate climate woollen tweed or angoras are, perhaps, the best general wear. For the sportsman, well dressed deer-skin is the best material, also mole-skin, canvas or karkee (coloured cotton).

Much of the traveller's comfort depends upon the capabilities of his servants.

A light heart can carry an elephant; a long face
stumbles under the weight of his turban.
Old Indian Saying

The most comfortable hose for travelling are thick, (not coarse) woollen socks. The tops should be sufficiently elastic to prevent slipping. They must fit well about the heel, so as to avoid blisters.

All experienced travellers seem to agree on one point, and that is the importance of wearing flannel next to the skin. No one who has any regard for his health will neglect the precaution of providing himself with shirts *and* under-clothing of this material, if he is at all likely to be exposed to sudden change of climate. It absorbs perspiration and prevents sudden chills.

In tropical climates, calico shirts may be worn, but without flannel under-clothing, linen should *never* be worn next to the skin.

PACKING

... properly directed and labelled ...

Always allow ample time for packing. Never omit to see for yourself that each portmanteau, valise or box is properly directed and labelled and that all labels previously used are removed.

When packing remember the saying; A little method is worth a great deal of memory.

The principal point to recollect in packing is to leave the things you are most likely to require, during the journey or on arrival at the first resting place, until last. If you carry a hand bag, small portmanteau or hold-all, they should be put in these.

The clothes least likely to be required should be packed first.

*When packing a trunk take care of the corners and the
centre will look after itself.*

HINTS RESPECTING BAGGAGE

1. Have your baggage carefully marked with your name and place of destination.

2. The premiums of insurance now paid are so small that it is well worth everybody's while to insure all baggage.

3. At the customs house be always ready and willing to open your portmanteau and you will then be generally treated politely and quickly despatched.

4. Steamer trunks should only be 12 inches deep so they can go beneath the berths in the cabin.

5. It is as well to make good use of a gentleman's remembrancer before and during the travelling.

$\mathcal{Q}$uestions of Travelling Etiquette

Should a man give up his seat to a woman in a crowded conveyance?

A courteous man has no hesitation in standing so that a lady may be seated.   It would not be expected of an extremely elderly man and a young man should be ready to offer his seat to an elderly man as well as to a lady.

Must a woman accept?

When offered a seat a woman should always accept it readily, with a smile and a word of thanks.   It is a slight to decline.

A CARPET BAG

... cram everything you want to take ...

Luggage - mark how the word hangs on the tongue. Was there ever a more expressive name?

Some say that if you want more than can be dropped into your coat pocket, then take a carpet bag. There is a popular tradition that a carpet bag will hold anything: we believe it. It can contain within itself an unknown quantity - just like a London omnibus!

Into this expansive receptacle cram everything you want to take, from a top coat to a tooth brush, and you always have a portable wardrobe at your disposal, that may at any time be swung from your hand, free from the extortionate grasp of the tavern porters!

UMBRELLA

To umbrella or not to umbrella, that is the question!!!

Your *true tourist* has no business with an umbrella. It gives a pre-supposition of everything that is damp!

BUT

It is said:

'It is the habitual carriage of the umbrella that is the stamp of respectability. The umbrella has become the acknowledged index of social position.'★

★J.W. Ferrier and R.L. Stevenson, The Philosophy of Umbrellas.

VISITING FRIENDS IN ENGLAND

*Trunks should have straps and stout brown
canvas covers.*

For ordinary travelling in England (if you
stay with friends) ladies will find it preferable to use
two medium dress baskets, rather than one large one.

In the firstplace, the size of your *one* box (if you
are a second or third class passenger) is liable to attract
the eyes of the porter who labels it and cause him to
weigh it, in which case it is seldom 'found wanting'!

In the second you run the risk of crushing your
dresses by packing boots and shoes in the same box.

In the third, at any house you go to where men
servants are not kept, women find a heavy trunk very
difficult to carry upstairs.

In the fourth place, you have only to see the
difficulty with which a servant girl and the driver get
your trunk on to a fly, to know what extra wear and
tear there is to your box in their efforts to hoist it up.

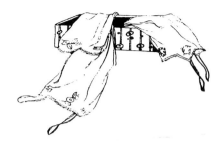

Dresses, blouses and lighter things should be packed in the larger bag.

Fold the skirts carefully right side out and put tissue paper between each fold and dress.

Put paper in the sleeves of the bodices to prevent crushing. Do not have too much spare space in your trunk otherwise clothes will shake down.

Jet or any kind of stone trimmings to garments should be covered in paper so that they do not mark other clothes.

It is a good plan to put at the top of each box what you are likely to want immediately on arrival.

The second trunk should take the hats, veils, and flowers in the tray if it is a strong one, so avoiding having a bonnet box. In the under part, pack all your boots, trees, shoes, linens etc.

The lightest and best boot trees are those sold at stores for less than two shillings a pair, that screw up to the size required.

In packing hats, put tissue paper into all bows, and plenty of paper between each hat, so they cannot shake about. If a bonnet box is preferred, the best kind is one of covered wicker, to the lining of which are added tapes, so that each hat can be firmly pinned to it, securing the feathers, lace or flowers, from any chance of being crushed.

An umbrella case, that will take your sunshades also, is useful; and if you must have a handbag, take one that you can carry yourself, only big enough to hold your book, newspaper, purse, and anything you may want on your journey.

The next essential is a stick - not a light, flimsy, fragile, fanciful cane for show, but a sound, seasoned, substantial stick.

See that all your bottles are tightly corked, and put each in one of the brown cardboard fluted wrappers used by chemists.

TONICS & RESTORATIVES

An important part of any luggage will be
1. Bicarbonate of Soda, to treat a burn or scald
2. Iodide of Potassium tablets, to treat colds in the head.
3. Quinine tablets, for colds accompanied by fever.
4. Cascara Sagrada tablets, for constipation.
5. Tablets of Soda Mint, to treat colic.
6. Peptonic tablets, for dispepsia or indigestion.

Tiger's milk is not a bad concoction for resuscitating the weary traveller. A reliable servant will have his own recipe and will carry the necessary spices.

Tiger's Milk Recipe
Beat yolks of six eggs with a modicum or half pint of spirit (rum or brandy) three lumps of sugar, a bit of lemon peel cut thin and a little spice such as cloves or cardamums. Add a quart of new milk, mix well, grating in some nutmeg. Enough for three people.

*Your railroad, when you come to understand it, is only
a device for making the world seem smaller.*
Ruskin.

THE RAILROAD

... safer to ride in ...

This new mode of transport should not be feared. It is safer to ride on the railroad than to walk through the streets and safer to ride in a railway carriage than in a perambulator, which is the safest of vehicles not driven by steam!

It is safer in a railway carriage than a perambulator
A perambulator is twice as safe as a dray,
five times as safe as an omnibus,
eight times as safe as a tramcar,
nine times as safe as a cab,
twelve times as safe as a carriage,
and ninety seven times as safe as a van or a cart!

There are usually separate carriages reserved for ladies who need to travel alone. **1885**

Questions of Travelling Etiquette

Is there any reason why I should not open the window in the railway compartment?

It is an unwritten law that the passengers occupying the window seats facing the engine have 'charge' of the windows. This is because they are most affected by the draught. There is no reason why you should not ask one of the window seat passengers if he would object to a window being opened.

PASSENGERS ON THE RAILWAY

*Avoid a number of small packages in the
railway carriage.*

You will always find amongst the passengers
a stout, ruddy faced, good humoured individual,
with a carpet bag slung upon one arm and a great coat
slung over the other who seems to be always treating
himself to railway excursions and bustling about the
station in the busiest and pleasantest manner imagi-
nable.

Another prominent feature is the lady who has
lost her bundle and who will always insist on looking
for it herself in the most unlikely and impossible
places.

Then there are sure to be two or three nervous
people - so overcome with awe at the immensity of
the railway station building that they perch themselves on the extreme edge of the bench.

*Q*uestions *of* Travelling Etiquette

Is it acceptable for a girl to make-up in public?

It is not a correct thing to do to make-up whilst travelling or in tea-rooms or cinemas. Many girls prefer not to reveal too openly how much their complexion owes to art instead of nature! Some young men are not altogether guiltless in this respect, for not infrequently one sees them vigorously using a comb or nail-file even at table.

There are many advantages of sea-travelling,
but security is not one of them.
Emerson

ON BOARD A STEAMER

Six golden rules ...

1. It is expected that the bedroom and table stewards and stewardesses and the 'Boots' should receive gratuities and the barber should be paid.
2. The servant should remember to take a deck chair with the owner's name on it. It is bad form to make a dash for the communal deck chairs.
3. The servant should pack a few linen bags in which to place combs and hair brushes and things generally put on the dressing table.
4. Pack plenty of woollen underclothing to last the voyage and a warm rug.
5. See to it that the window is about an inch open at the top when sleeping but make sure there is no draught across the bed.
6. The servant should always carry a supply of coppers and small silver with him to reward excellent service.

$\mathcal{Q}$uestions of Travelling Etiquette

What tip should one leave on a cruising holiday?

You will be doing the right thing if you give an amount equal to ten per cent of your passage cost - £2 on a trip of £20 and so on. Your cabin steward and dining-room steward should receive the major portion of the sum.

LOST? THEN USE YOUR WATCH!

Every watch is a compass.

Point the hour to the sun and the south is exactly half way between the hour and the figure 12 on the watch. For instance, suppose it is 4 o'clock, point the hand indicating 4 to the sun and 2 on the watch will be exactly south.

Three useful items to remember:
a barometer, a telescope and a pocket sextant.

PATIENCE AND GOOD HUMOUR

Do not think yourself specially neglected if waiters at hotels do not bring what you call for in double-quick time. Nothing so distinctly marks the well-bred as patience on such occasions.

Always keep in mind that the enjoyment of travelling, like other pleasures, must be purchased at some little expense, and he whose good humour can be ruffled by every petty inconvenience he may encounter had unquestionably better remain at home!

The traveller should adapt himself to the customs and ideas of the people in whose country he so-journs. He should always be a gentleman in his actions, never in his pretensions and his real worth will become apparent, even amongst foreigners.

KEEPING A JOURNAL

Pack a good writing case ...

Many experienced voyagers keep a journal while they are travelling. A well kept journal acts as a remembrancer for years to come.

Be sure to pack a good writing case with inks, nibs blotters and note pads.

UP IN THE AIR

Ballooning started in 1783. Parachuting in 1797. Parachuting tower-jumpers have fixed artificial wings to themselves and jumped into space - often proving that they couldn't fly!

Sir George Cayley laid down the basis of the science of aerodymanics and can be called the 'Father of Aeronautical Navigation' but Wilbur and Orville Wright were the first to conquer the air in 1903.

On July the twenty-fifth 1909 Louis Bleriot succeeded in his flight across the English Channel.

'The time will come when gentlemen, when they were to go a journey, will call for their wings as regularly as they called for their boots.'

Up in a balloon, boys up in a balloon,
All among the stars, sailing round the moon;
Up in a balloon, boys, up in a balloon
It's something very jolly to be up in a balloon'
H P Farnie Up in a Balloon.

'Down the sea path I wound to the sea shore
The evening was most clear and beautiful,
And there the sea I found,
Calm as a sleepy child in sleepless slumber bound.'
Shelley

AT THE SEA-SIDE

... there is not a luxury in nature to compare with it

A bathing machine is an aquatic caravan containing two towels, two ricketty hat pegs, a damp flooring, a strong smell of sea-weed, and a broken looking glass, exhibiting the phenomena of oblique refraction.

To rise betimes of a bright summer morning, to invest oneself negligently in loose, cool and comfortable clothing to walk steedily to the sea-side, to undress in one of these amphibious vehicles, whilst the music of the waves dashing against the wheels, or gurgling through the crannies in the wooden steps, greets your delighted ears - to plunge henceforemost into the sea sparkling in the rays of the rising sun - then to resume our left-off clothing and feel the ecstatic glow exhilarating the whole frame, is the apex of enjoyment - there is not a luxury in nature to compare with it!

Then the ladies with their flowing sea-dresses and their curiously close caps - to see them cautiously stepping down the little stairs of the machine into the arms of two aquatic gentlewomen who receive them. Whish! Flop! There's a plunge beneath the onward rolling wave.

Every holiday at the sea should begin with a spell of laziness. 'Overplay' is as dangerous an ailment as overwork and it is wise to let the concluding part of the holiday be spent restfully too. A time of laziness on pier or promenade well winds up the annual recess!

Another pleasant pastime, peculiar to marine excursionists, is the collection of shells and seaweed gathering on the beach. The best time to search on the sea shore is at the new or full moon, for then the tide makes great ebb and the collector should be on the shore two hours before low water.

'It is perhaps a more fortunate destiny
to have a taste for collecting shells than
to be born a millionaire'
R L Stevenson

Questions of Travelling Etiquette

What is the correct way to behave on the continent?

The old phrase 'When in Rome do as Rome does,' provides the required guidance. When foreigners come to Britain we expect them to conform to our usages and customs so we should do the same in foreign lands. The code of courtesy is the same everywhere but the continentals are more effusive and demonstrative. One respect in which British tourists fail frequently is in the lack of proper respect for continental churches, which they treat as show places.

TRAVELLING ON THE CONTINENT

To some people a tea-basket is indispensable

In travelling abroad you may want to consider taking as little luggage as possible in the railway carriage.

To keep costs down, you may consider keeping your heaviest things in bags or hold-alls in the carriage with you, much to the annoyance of everyone!

Or you may wish to travel very comfortably, pay the price and put all you can in the van, and take as little as possible in the carriage.

This little *must* consist of a Gladstone bag, in one side of which all things required for a night's use can be put, so as to avoid more packing than necessary for an early start.

A case must be taken for sunshades and
umbrellas, a fur-lined cloak in straps and
a handbag you can carry yourself sufficiently
large to take just what you may want on a
journey, including an air cushion which
folds into a small space, towel, soap,
sponge, nailbrush and comb, for
use if travelling at night.

To some people a tea-basket is indispensable, but to avoid carrying an extra package the tea things can be packed in the trunk. You can take half a pound of tea leaf each person through the custom house free of tax. Continental tea can sometimes be very bad!

One of the great causes of sickness in tropical climates is bad water. However, although the traveller ought to make the rule not to drink any that has not been previously boiled or filtered, he ought to take great care that he is offering no offence.

Beware of packing valuable jewellery in trunks on the long continental journeys for fear of theft. Do not take more jewellery than you can carry on your person. Some people prefer to take costume jewellery only, leaving their gems safely with the bankers at home.

Boxes should have good locks and a strong canvas cover
to lessen the risk of them being
tampered with.

Hints On Packing, by An Old Traveller

Comply cheerfully and gracefully with the customs of the conveyances in which you travel, and of the places where you stop.

WINTERING ABROAD

These important points of etiquette are particularly useful for those wintering abroad and therefore indulging in social visits.

1. The gentleman should be introduced to the lady, but if the sexes are the same, always present the inferior in rank to the superior.

2. Before presenting a gentleman to a lady, always obtain permission.

3. Acknowledge an introduction by a bow, not by offering the hand.

4. Letters of introduction should be given to bearers unsealed. The bearer should send them to the addressee by post, enclosing his own card.

5. Afternoon calls are usually made between the hours of two and four.

6. A gentleman should take his hat into the room with him, holding it in his hand during the visit.

WINTERING ABROAD

7. Visits should not exceed half an hour.

8. Avoid looking at your watch during a call.

9. If, during a visit, a lady caller leaves it is polite to rise.

10. On other visitors arriving, wait until they are seated, then leave, previously bowing to the newly arrived callers.

11. If walking with a friend, you are met or joined by another it is unnecessary to introduce one to the other.

12. In conversation with persons of rank avoid frequent use of their title. Address them as sir or madam.

13. Never interrupt a person when speaking.

14. Do not make a display of wit.

15. Whispering, or speaking in a language all are not acquainted with, is in bad taste.

16. Scandal under no circumstances should be indulged in.

THE MANY DIFFERENT TOURISTS

The grumbling tourist

– grumbles about leaving his own mansion, yet goes away without the expectation of being more comfortable elsewhere. He always complains – the beds are too hard, bills too long, time too short, dishes too sweet, wines too sour etc.

The gastronomic tourist

– looks on the world as a large larder and every country as a distinct shelf! He'll go to Yarmouth for bloaters, Cambridge for sausages, Colchester for oysters and the South Downs of Sussex for mutton!

The philanthropic tourist

– prides himself on the possession of a large heart, but forgets that, like a large purse, it is no use without its being well filled – and he does not give himself time to understand.

The begging tourist

– gathers in a harvest wherever he goes and never travels but he gleans something. From every town he must carry a sample of the most famous characteristic. At every stop he takes you may hear him say – 'I shall be so happy to retain this as a souvenir of my visit'.

The sentimental tourist

– haunts ruined abbeys by twilight and bathes himself in moonlight. He writes limping sonnets to venerable farms under the impression of their being castles of antiquity and gets very ecstatic about morning and very sleepy about night. He will throw himself into a reverie before an old monastery and he folds his arms in thought!

The adventurous tourist

– never comes to a new locality without wanting a new excitement. A night in a haunted chamber or an encounter with the brigands would give him most intense gratification.

MERELY FOR
THE SAKE OF TRAVELLING

Tourists are volatile and evanescent – no sooner here than there, never seeming to rest for more than five minutes!

For some, the great aim seems to be the solution of a mathematical problem, which involves the getting over the greatest possible amount of ground in the smallest amount of time! He goes off like a sky rocket – the period of his return is about as uncertain as that of the last newly-discovered comet. Such is a tourist who merely travels for the sake of travelling.

He may have drunk champagne in goblets on the Rhine and sipped his *Kirchenwasser* on the Alps – he may have quaffed burgundy in Paris and soothed himself with sherbet in Turkey, swallowed his sherry on the top of Trajan's pillar and hobbed and nobbed brandy over the heights of Chimborazo, or sucked a Sherry Cobbler under the Falls of Niagara.

In travelling we improve imperceptibility,
not in the head only, but in the heart.
Our prejudices leave us; seas and mountains
are no longer our boundaries; we learn to
love, to esteem and to admire beyond them.
Our benevolence extends itself with our
knowledge and we return
better than we went!

THE CUSTOMS HOUSE

His nose detects the two bottles ...

Custom house officials can always be recognised by their physiognomy. The eye is a piercer, the nose a note of interrogation, the mouth a volcanic crater, dreadful for curiosity to contemplate.

When he looks upon a conscious contrabandist you feel the glance dart diametrically through the fourth button of your vest and come burning its way out, the other side. His nose detects the two bottles of Eau de Cologne, the fraudulent flask of cognac or the surreptitious cigar!

A LIST OF DUTIABLE GOODS 1893.

Tobacco,
cigars,
wines, ale, beer,
playing cards,
chicory,
currants in essence of spruce,
figs and fig cake,
preserved fruits in spirits,
naphtha pickles,
plums, prunes, raisins,
ether, iodine` of ethyl,
chloroform, cologne water, varnish.

Science will in a few years abolish all this absurdity
of passport carrying and exhibiting.
Edward Blanchard 1855

TRAVELLING HISTORY

Travellers in antiquity were a rarity and were regarded with great respect.

There were men who travelled over Europe and Asia with more the spirit of the modern traveller like Sir John de Mandeville who was born about 1300 in St. Albans and visited Egypt, the Holy Land and China amongst other places. His history of these travels was one of the very earliest books printed in this country.

Travel through the nations of western Europe began about the time of the crusades. The pilgrimages and crusades of the Middle Ages were the forefathers of the modern tours.

TRAVELLING HISTORY

When stage coaches first appeared on the road it is no easy matter to determine. In 1662 we find six making slow and anything but sure journeys to the West and North of England. These were looked on as presumptuous attempts 'to rival the flight of birds.'

At the close of the 18th century travelling became the fashion. It was the correct thing to do the Grand Tour of Europe for all persons of rank. They set out on a regular and methodical visit to the European capitals. The 'masses' couldn't do this because of the expense and the time involved.

Railways and steamers have changed all this bringing the possibility of travel to most people, if they were willing to travel 2nd and 3rd class!

TRAVELLING HISTORY

In 1842 a train of 110 vehicles, with four engines in front, and one pushing behind, brought the people back from Edinburgh after seeing the Queen.

In 1885 for a tour including travelling expenses and hotel in the nearer parts of the continent, viz. North of France, Belgium, Holland, Switzerland etc.. you may allow about 15 shillings a day – for Italy, Eastern Germany, Bohemia allow £1 and for Scandinavia 18 shillings.

THE ETIQUETTE COLLECTION
Collect the set!

ETIQUETTE FOR COFFEE LOVERS
Fresh coffee - the best welcome in the world!
Enjoy the story of coffee drinking,
coffee etiquette and recipes.

ETIQUETTE FOR CHOCOLATE LOVERS
Temptation through the years.
A special treat for all Chocolate Lovers.

THE ETIQUETTE OF NAMING THE BABY
A good name keeps its lustre in the dark.
Old English Proverb

THE ETIQUETTE OF ENGLISH PUDDINGS
Traditional recipes for good old-fashioned
puddings - together with etiquette notes for serving.

ETIQUETTE FOR GENTLEMEN
*"If you have occasion to use your handkerchief
do so as noiselessly as possible."*

Copper Beech Book makes the perfect gift. We also publish books
about parlour games, servants, graphology and social secrets.

THE ETIQUETTE COLLECTION
Collect the set!

THE ETIQUETTE OF AN ENGLISH TEA
How to serve a perfect English afternoon tea;
traditions, superstitions, recipes and how to read your
fortune in the tea-leaves afterwards.

THE ETIQUETTE OF POLITENESS
Good sense and good manners.
How to be polite and well-bred at all times.

THE ETIQUETTE OF DRESS
Fashion tips from bygone days.

THE ETIQUETTE OF LOVE AND COURTSHIP
A guide for romantics.
Flirting, temptation, first impressions:
essential advice for lovers.

For your free catalogue containing these and other Copper Beech
Gift Books, write to:

Copper Beech Publishing Ltd
P O Box 159 East Grinstead Sussex England RH19 4FS

Copper Beech Gift Books
are designed and printed
in Great Britain.